1981

OUT OF THE DESERT

OUT OF THE DESERT

Poems by Diane Levenberg

DOUBLEDAY & COMPANY, INC., GARDEN CITY, NEW YORK 1980

Grateful acknowledgment is made to the following:

To Alvin Wainhaus
So much of your music is in these poems

To Jeff Oboler
We've shared many dreams   This book is one of them

Out of the Desert originally appeared in *Earths Daughters: a feminist arts periodical.* Reprinted by permission. *The Wandering Jew* originally appeared in *The Jewish Spectator.* Reprinted by permission. *The Wedding* and *The Crippler* appeared in *Lilith,* the independent Jewish feminist magazine, published at 250 West 57th Street, New York, New York 10019. Copyright © 1976, 1977 Lilith Publications, Inc. All rights reserved. *Rosh Hashanah Love Poem* originally appeared in *The National Jewish Monthly.* Reprinted by permission. *After Selecting the Wedding Invitations* and *Dreaming of Conn-Eda* from *New Poets: Women: An Anthology,* copyright © 1976 by Les Femmes Publishing, Millbrae, California 94030. Reprinted by permission. *A Jewess Learns to Meditate, Alchemy, Friday Night, Tisha b'Av 1974, My Eastern Madness, My Friday Night Man, Chanukah 1975,* and *The Death of My Messiah* appeared in *Response* magazine, Department of Sociology, Queens College, Flushing, New York 11367.
Adapted excerpt from *I Know Your Heart, Marco Polo* by Henry Bromell. Reprinted by permission of Alfred A. Knopf, Inc. Excerpt from Heinrich Zimmer, *The King and the Corpse,* ed. Joseph Campbell, Bollingen Series XI, copyright 1948, © 1957 by Princeton University Press, copyright © (renewed) 1975 by Princeton University Press. *The Red Wheelbarrow* from *The Collected Earlier Poems of William Carlos Williams,* copyright 1938 by New Directions Publishing Corporation. Permission to reprint this poem set differently from the original granted by New Directions. Excerpt from *Do not go gentle into that good night* from *Collected Poems of Dylan Thomas.* Copyright 1952 by Dylan Thomas. Reprinted by permission of New Directions and J. M. Dent and Sons, Ltd., London.

ISBN: 0-385-15236-1 Library of Congress Catalog Card Number 79-7113 Copyright © 1980 by Diane Levenberg All Rights Reserved Printed in the United States of America First Edition

For my mother Miriam Sima bas Lena
Through these poems at last we speak

For Florence Miale my ideal reader
Only then did this work begin

For Judy Schmidt
Who showed me that with love there is poetry even
in our most everyday act of life

CONTENTS

OUT OF THE DESERT

The Night They Accepted My Book

The night they accepted my book
I had dinner with my adulterous lover
who is himself an important man
and therefore only gets jealous
when on the nights he goes home
to his wife
my unmarried lover stays over

The night they accepted my book
I had a drink
with my first woman analyst
who after the silent ones
and the seducers
began to call me a poet
We talked of drive and dedication

The night they accepted my book
I had tea
with my current therapist
I shared a poem with her
and some friends
about light and creating and the

passion of trying to put that
into painted words

The night they accepted my book
I came home alone
grabbed my pillow
asked my dead mother
if she were finally proud of me
and cried myself to sleep

I

Was it sunny / When you died?

The Apartment

Because I had never
Cleaned before
It wasn't mine
Was the excuse

(My stepmother
Hid my mother's pictures
Her double bed
Hid the livingroom
I left home at twelve
and have walked on tiptoe
Until these rooms)

I rub my hands
Into the wood
Bare feet on the tiles
Laying into every corner
Wanting it to absorb
My self   my smell
Mine

These Bones

Blood on the door-post
Everyone passed by
Inside the angel of death
A woman who wouldn't
Let me sleep
In the morning when
Sometimes in the garden
I would play with my box of memory bones

The children would come
Blowing their wind flowers
Until the time to weave their
Daisy chain around me chanting
Dead your mother's dead
You are dancing on her grave I'd scream
Box in hand running to the

Cellar cool damp and dirty
The only sound the furnace
The flames
This is the place the babies were thrown
How did they grow to dance in my garden

The pipes would echo
My thumping heart to the kitchen
And in answer I could hear the laughter of
Athaliah* my stepmother's daughter

In the kitchen the sun
Reflected from the gold lattice
On the windows woven by the spiders
Ordered by my father to keep me in
The yellow-handled bread knife
An extension of her hand
Athaliah laughs again

New blood is wanted for the door-post
The scars on my right arm have never healed
Our mother walks in
Her red and black flannel
Darkens the room
Drinking my blood
I have seen you playing in the garden

My breakfast is oatmeal
Sprinkled with the dust of my memory bones

* Athaliah: Jezebel's daughter

The Crippler

"Many resorted to self-mutilation to render themselves unfit for
military service. They chopped off their fingers or toes,
damaged their eyesight, and perpetrated every possible form
of maiming. . . . The most tender-hearted mother . . . would
place the finger of her beloved son under the kitchen knife of
a home-bred quack surgeon."

S. M. Dubnow. *History of the
Jews in Russia and Poland*

In Kherson Russia we had The Crippler
Cataracts of despair in two rheumy caverns
Himself a crippled craftsman
Working by the always burning *yahrzeit* candle
His tortuous hands now palsied and pained

The trees of the forest surrounding us
Guarding his wounded hut
Silent sentries observing this patient line
(That same line always repeated
Mournful refrain through cry-filled centuries
Ani Maamin   Eli Eli)

Mothers holding children in terror-filled grip
The Crippler the means to keep
Their sons at home

These children would not fight
In the Czar's conscript army
Would not serve as Cantonist
A minimum of twenty years
"Bring the boy" he whispers
Vising shivering child
Blind hands encompassing
Face   arms   legs   waist
"Two fingers on the right hand"
Bring the next boy
Caressing face   arms   legs
The right foot to be
Bent forever out of shape
The Crippler works quickly

I watch ten boys
Enter the room whole
I hear ten boys and
Their screams are echoed still
My turn and The Crippler
Examines my face
Sifts my hair
I feel holes in my body
Fathered by his touch

"A girl" he whispers
"Why a girl
I have never . . .

Not a girl"
"Do it" my mother hisses
"Do it
A whore in the Czar's army
To couple with *goyim*
Never will it be this one
The rabbi's daughter"

He cuts my hair
Crosses an eye
Pours lead in my left leg
And my face slowly freezes
Into the ugliness of this agony
"My mother is dead
This is my father's jealous wife'
I scream to be heard
But in the windowless room
I stand alone amid a
Minyan of maimed boys
And The Crippler continues
A Khazarian thrust and
The blood between my legs
Adds to the pool slowly
Wasting the wood of the floor

Years later we hear of The Healer
Some never reach her and for

Five years I search
Half the world
The old woman
Like the Witch of Endor
Necromances the soul
To spirit the body
My hair has grown back
We are still working on the leg
I still walk very slowly
My gaze is steady   fixed
In fact at times
I can look right through you

But the heart is beyond
The work of The Healer
and the heart still cries
It may never stop
The Healer has advised
"But this heart" she added
"Pumps both blood and tears"

The Scream That Doesn't End

Tighter
And tighter
I'm ready to snap

She snapped
They told me
After my brother was born
My mother
        snapped

Postpartum depression
A name for the pine-needle pillow
She made for me then
You can't sleep on pine needles
You can only smell them

She came home later
To die in the morning
Was it sunny
When you died
Or did the rain
Make you long for the damp earth?

My throat is so raw
From the scream that doesn't
                              end
I long to reach into the
                          cool earth
And kiss from it your blood
I walk the streets
                   and gr-r-r

Who is pulling?
They tell me
I've made it up
And whatever undoes it
I cannot have
They are even cruel enough
                           to say
I do not want it

The analyst said
Take dancing lessons
                     or
Remember what you dream
This will help you
                   he said
To know who you are
Before the tightness
Snaps you in half

Or in thirds
Or as many people
As you think
                    you are
On a given day
Who is pulling?
You are too dead to hear

If I don't snap-to . . .

Friday Night

They had something those Jews
who went out to take in
their double portion a day
of rest beginning with a
Friday night gift I've
long since exchanged

Just before sunset it begins to
hurt and each week a homesickness for
a different kind of home begins
and I choose again and again
to try to ignore it

Friday night meant sitting
with my young father and mother
by the light of the candles all
of us very quiet and even then
I wanted to know if I could break
through the walls of my grapefruit
both of them laughing gently at
a child they loved

Friday night then and now is
Russian music   *challah* crumbs
in the pages of a *Jewish Folklore*
A cello concerto in minor
lights candles in the kitchen
a dim bulb in the bathroom
and one soft reading light near
the living room couch and I
try to escape this 5,000 year old
tradition in a grimy bar
the only connection to my Friday night
is that I'm still drinking wine

To My Mother

We are lying naked
in a pink Parisian twilight
I put us in Paris
because it is in that city
that all the permutations
of love are acceptable

I could however bring us
just as easily to Jerusalem
though there I clothe you
in a moon white cotton caftan
In the dying summer light
we lie entwined
as the blood of pomegranates
streaks across the sky

If we remain in Paris
I tell you   my mother
that the first time
we made love
as he came inside me
he cried, *"Ma mère"*

You smile and remind me
that all little deaths
lead us to embrace our needs

Sometime during that purple Parisian night
I offer you a line
from my first adulterous poem
Desdemona's eyes were oh so green
And now so are yours
You whisper in reply
"When he assures you
that your eyes are mad
tell him that like maggots
they have eaten away
at bits of my heart"

If we embrace in Jerusalem
I tell you that for me
the sounds of mother
all mean truth
Emet   Om   Emah
You say nothing
In the light of my ancient truth
I cry Mother   Mother
I almost killed myself
to find you

II

We wrestle / Into a love act / That solves nothing

The Satin Horn Is Playing

The satin horn is playing
there is no hair on your body
With you I am thin enough
to slip through keyholes

His emery thighs hide arrows
His desire has no resin
Your satin horn is playing
and here there are emeralds

Now our coda is crude
We are thin enough
to sneak through keyholes
But at the bottom
my stone is the ruby
yours the skimmer

Love Poem

What I finally wanted
Was conversation in your bed
Passion now
Alchemized to intellect
(Instead you slept)

I had almost told you
Just before that moment
How much I loved you

On Such Stuff As Dreams Are Made

Lying on him afterward
A hook-nosed Jewess
Dreams of her kinky hair
Straightening in the rain
Instead of the reverse

It's his elbow now
Instead of fleshy hollow
She wakens
Breathing heavily
Their act is hard to follow

Descending from bed
Walking nude
To the bathroom mirror
There—her face as sad as ever

Because he calls her
Lovely
She goes back to hear him snore

Keep the Mandrakes

You do not accept me
Speaking of this
We wrestle

Into a love act
That solves nothing
You are pained

Jacob's angel
Kneed *him* in the groin

Looking for the Ruby

Here in your arms a crying child
Every time I make love
I am an orphan
Looking for the ruby my mother swallowed
For the pearl my father keeps
Locked between his teeth

Open your mouth and give me jewels
Open your heart and let me know
That what keeps me crying
Is in the music
Not at all in you

This music   this Friday night
This 1940's man who tells me
"She took my manhood"
This woman in me
Who wants to give it back

A warm red ecstasy is for
Different kinds of lovers
Open your mouth

I will share with you my toys
In 1940 Frankie Laine
Sang haunting refrains
In 1971 you make modern love
And tell me that you like me

What happened in the 40's
Is that on a Friday night
My mother felt this music
Asked my father to hold her
In his narrow bed
And gave him a daughter

What happens here is that
I can give you nothing back
Of what she took
You give me a pleasant way
To fall asleep
Then turn off the music
And go home to your wife

Cocksure

"Come on" he said
drunkenly
holding her hand
on his stiffened penis
"you know
I'm hard
to get"

"But not"
she said
sober
and demurely
releasing her hand
"hard
to come by"

To My Husband on Being Accepted by a School
of Social Work

As a little girl in a small town movie theater
surrounded by ghosts and silhouettes
I became totally entranced by the
man on the screen in a tee shirt shaving
while his wife at the bathroom door
argued laughed cried (I don't remember any more)

Years later after visiting a sick friend
lying on a beach surrounded by my darkness
and his imminent death
I saw the man again
in a tee shirt horn-rimmed glasses
Mazel Tov a happy dream
and if not for my analyst
would have promptly forgotten it

This morning there was a new man
shaving   whistling   dancing through the kitchen
His tee shirt as I lay my head against it
smelled comfortingly of sweat and spice

Through the horn-rimmed glasses his eyes
told me my childhood movie star
underdressed groom of a Miami dream
without a doubt had arrived

My Eastern Madness

Walking with you
sleeping with you
I am in Jerusalem
facing the water
Impossible you say
Jerusalem has no shore

This is how my worlds combine
On an island
in a Byzantine city
whose banks have overflowed
with ripened pomegranates

You are a reincarnated soul
a Sephardic holy woman
dressed in long brocade and David's gold
You hosted hundreds at your table

Were we lovers then
the Sephardic lonely woman
the innocent Yavneh scholar

who graced my palace with Solomon's words
seduced me with a long forgotten balalaika tune

Impossible you say
Jerusalem has no water
and we had no such past
Goodnight my love
Sing to me one more time
Lead me to the house of wine
and let me have my Eastern madness

My Friday Night Man

Who could have come here
juggling challahs in the air
Lighting candles
by blowing kisses
through the open door

You are my Friday night man
take Chagall's fiddler
give him a guitar
and there you are my darling
there you are

Who could have come here
magically filling goblets
with one Chassidic song
offering me Sabbath rest
by spiraling me
along your arabesque

You are my Friday night man
take Chagall's fiddler
give him a guitar
and there you are my darling
there again you are

Tisha b'Av 1976*

They say that tonight
the Messiah may be born
And as I lie in your arms
I know that as men
may have wished to be the Messiah
(even as you my dear
have once or twice thought
of saving the world)
I at least would like to think
that perhaps I could be
the one to bear him forth
(Like the best of us
like Ruth
I could if I had to
link my genealogy to David)

Lying in your arms however
what I bear is pain
I see you looking past me
towards Jerusalem's most humble gate

* Fast day celebrated on the ninth day of the Jewish month of Av com-
memorating the destruction of the Temple of Jerusalem.

wondering if you are man enough
to take that perilous ride
I want not the infant Messiah
but Messiah the man
And if tonight
as my deliverer he came
I would unbind his wounds
and lie with him
as now with you
(Ah, how we women
find a way to bless the coming)

Now please hold me
for if tonight cannot yet be
the night that he is born
(I grant no other woman
that selfsame right)
perhaps in a moment filled with
universal pain and private ecstasy
he may be through our troubled love conceived

Chanukah 1975

Eight days to think about
my desperate need for heroes
Judah, hammer my heart
Judith, Holofernes is *here*
offer me enough wine
to forget the enmity
of lonely lightings
Simon, in this solstice
give me rest
from all my private festivals
dedicated to imaginary holocausts
Ubiquitous Maccabees
purify my modern desecrations

Stand higher
Shine brighter
Offer nothing
but the pleasure of your presence
Eight days of laughter
hold the secret

Yet now I tell you
I fear these heroes
their deeds so pure
they extinguish my own fires
These heroes
with their acts so daring
they might consume my life

Chanukah 1976

Well, love I'd almost thought
we'd lost it
already these seven nights
had passed in darkness

How kind
these solstice nights are longest
and we are here
a celebration of passionate shadows
caught within our menorah's
ancient fire

Reality, love
offers its own miracle
while we two shadows
must learn to rest content
within its patient cosmic glow

Rosh Hashanah Love Poem

It was 3:00 in the morning
and at that hour
the tasks of the day
had married us

The kitchen was steamy
with the scent of food
You came in to stick
your scholar's nose
in my holiday pot
"So this is how
you make a roast"—
stabbing at potatoes
tasting gravy   cutting tiny bites of meat

You were preparing your sermon
and asked me to interpret
an Aggadic metaphor
What I wanted you to know
was that those moments were the metaphor
All I wanted from New Year sweetness
All I wanted of my

talents and yours
blending and feeding each other
What I wanted you to know
That hour those moments
were also for my mother—
she and *her* rabbi never content
never together as I was then with you

So we talked with passion
and Talmudic precision
about metaphors
and the inadequacy of figures of speech
and then, love, you made
the most appropriate gesture
and there was the taste of apples
in your mouth

Jung and I at Bollingen

It is twilight in the Alps
a kind of cosmic comfort
infuses both our lives
For us it is near the end
Offer your fire another log Jung
More warmth is needed
in this last of our Swiss winters

Outside the purple Alps
intensifies the fever in my blood
you have conquered every Matterhorn
and though you say it doesn't matter
I shall never climb your mountains
Ah   Jung the figure in your carpet
is the whole twentieth century
And all I can do
like a naive African native
is pray upon it

Time preys on both of us
Against the small of your broad back
I dream again

You turn and say
Try this skullcap on for size
Your ring brushes against my forehead
There is I tell you
more light in this tower
than I and my world can bear
When the lightning strikes
you will be dead
and tomorrow all I will hear
is the dying song of logs burning

The Death of My Messiah

It takes time to plan a murder
I need time
to touch his hair (mine)
caress his eyes (mine)
slide my lips along
his happy mouth (yours)
play my fingers
beneath his chin (yours)
I know just how he looks
and what he might become
occupies my wildest fantasies
For this I need the time

Would he teach me
how to get from here to there
or stammer his way through eternity
My son stopping suns
or translating our legacy
of word and song
into his gift for poignant psalms
Perhaps he might become

the son of the David in my dreams
offering all of us a destiny
we might at last respect

It takes time to plan a murder
destroy a destiny
as it took us time
to learn to love
only ourselves

The Passion of Light

for Judy

You are sitting in a rocking chair
the muted light intimating
perfect shadows across your face
You are wearing orange
When Modigliani saw that color
he tried to blend it with the pink
of a terra cotta dawn he thought he knew
But still there was someone
wearing that orange in a perfect light
So he drugged himself to death

I am telling you that all day
I have been in a place
where the light is pure and blinding
filled only with a diamond space
and some small comfort of my own presence

Here the memory of that light
becomes flames burning the space
between my breasts
Here I am offered another light

waves of it
shuddering across your face
And every time I close my eyes
or take a breath
it melts

I am telling you of my fear
of committing my life to metaphors
You quietly cover your lap
with a wool of green and blue
When van Gogh saw those colors
he bled them with the sea and sky
of his own tormented soul
and still there was someone
dressed in green and blue
So he sent a yellow bullet
through his chest

Some books should make us
feel, said Kafka
as though we're on the verge of suicide
I am telling you that the story of my life
lies still half-written on my desk
and of the light never as now
never right enough to give it life
What Beethoven must have gone through
to create in his Pastorale

the spectacle of lightning
On his deathbed
begging his private god
to let him hear
one well-played upward stroke

In this attic room
the light is passing from its source
painting you and binding us
"That I would write myself
into this scene I had never doubted
But that someone else would help me
create it—that I had never suspected"
And my hands stay locked behind my back
so this flame of light has room
to burn the space between my breasts

In another room
not nearly half as light as yours
I try again
Modigliani paints my fingers orange
van Gogh brushes my lips with sunflowers
and Beethoven grants me
one upward stroke
What you hold in your hand
is the passion of light

III

All that time wasted/wandering the Sinai of/
my false idea

On the Way to My Analyst's Office

for Florence who is
always there
when I get there

. . . And if it's all a mistake
Just a junkie with a
cluttered life on my way
to a psychic fix I
will roll up my sleeves
and unleash a dream

. . . And if there is no
becoming isn't this the
terrible failure of my being
What can she answer
her "no" just a false
smile on the face
of a cellophane bag

For three dollars in
the plastic church basement
of the Ansonia Hotel there

is a psychic who answers
three questions but what
would I dare to ask her and
could I stop going for more

Alchemy

Friday afternoon: chicken eggs
soaking on the drainboard   (for soup)
My mother in our sunny pantry
grinding liver   wiping perspiration
with her apron   brief Yiddish
phrases in hurried phone conversations

Six years of watching these
before-the-Sabbath preparations
nourishing me through the next nineteen
(A Jewish mother's suicide:
It's all right   there's a box of farina
in the cupboard
and a jar of chicken soup
in the Frigidaire)

Twenty years later
the same smell of onions
I had almost forgotten the magic
of *gribinis* in rendered chicken fat
hard boiled eggs   chicken livers
and a Jewish mother to transform them

You remind me
(suddenly a six-year-old again)
it's the wrong day   (Sunday)
the liver hasn't been salted
and while my mother
took frequent sips of phone conversation
you are drinking whiskey and water

Yet this feminine alchemy—you
feeding me golden onions from your fingers
as I gratefully watch the rest
become my private eucharist

I remind you that
my mother knew I would watch you
prepare this tasty dish
taste of it
and feel loved and whole again

Jung and I

Having a dialogue with Jung who
speaks so eloquently in his
tender masculinity
Man and His Symbols: a crowned her-
maphrodite strikes further revelations
on an archetypal chord

Male and Female residing side
by side and rightly so and I a
troubled woman know the problem
Light hits the page just as
colors reflecting hard hit notes
Miles Davis blowing his heart out
lonely *canto hondo* of the trumpet and
it all comes together

A Jewess Learns to Meditate

Every special event has its ceremony
This I learned
From years of adolescent ritual

O ma shanti ananda
So I thought I heard
Barauch ata shehechianu
So I wanted to hear

On her knees
Gotunyu
They told me it wasn't religious
I will refuse to kneel . . .
Got tzudanken
(Strange the occasions my Yiddish
chooses to return)
No one asks me to

My mantra is somehow
Evoked and offered in circles of sound
Along its radius I hear a Hebrew word
And know therefore I will

Never forget it
"It is easy?"
Face East
Keep your feet together
Bend the knees
Bow the head

Eighteen Hebrew prayers in which to meditate
And not one ever worked
What rabbi ever learned to ask
"It is easy?"

My secret mantra
Modeh ani
I thank you for my mantra
The incense burning
Spices!   *Havdalah!*
End *Shabbos* End

Forgotten God
(I meditate without my mantra)
Don't get upset
At this heretical question
You and I both know that lately
Most whys addressed to You
Are petrified echoes
Are merely post-holocaust rhetoric

You had them teach me
Shemone Esrai
Modeh Ani
Which frightened me
Lest I forget
Lest *I* forget
(Meditating with my mantra)
Lest *you* forget
How your right hand
Shovelled like so much coal
A generation of Jews
From creation to cremation
Our history

Why is it
How come
A Hebrew sounding word
Brings back old times—
A word with You
And pages of prayer books
Might as well have remained blank

Modeh ani lefanecha
In the mornings meditating
I thank you
For my mantra
May the spirit of the East
Our differences transcend

Nomenclature

Nomenclature
The Soho artist
Scribbles on the drawing paper
A loosening up of the wrist
The portrait is suddenly beautiful
My face romanticized
Within the candles' charcoal glow
Drawn from the dead
My mother's face
Suffers righteously

Not mine
Were this face mine
Were your name mine
Were your care-filled
Dark-eyed Bible name mine
My suffering would be sensuous
Pain worn proudly in the womb
What a woman knowingly feels
What the world always senses
Instead: I am clownish, foolish
Self-consciously weighted down

You, Miriam—weighing only ninety pounds
Gliding eloquently into
Unconscious absence—
Miriam—lovely, serene
Your face mysteriously
Tonight in my hands

You could succeed in such escape
I survive
And seek from you
No answers
Only: there might have been
A different heritage to have left me
I survive
And seek from you
No answers
Another name

Pope Pius XII Sees a Star of David

Montini entered at noon
"The letter, Your Holiness"
The letter
Nine months delayed
postmarked Istanbul
July 8, 1943

The heir to the See of Peter
read it
rolled a cigarette
(a habit he had adopted
from Hadrian)
smoked it on the balcony
My kingdom is of this world
all of Rome. . . .

Pacing his private chamber
sanctum sanctorum
he stroked his cross—
it offered his fingers no idea
fondled his rosary—
it glowed no answer

But then and there
the papal robe
showed blood
a bleeding Star of David

In an arc of light
above the window
he saw their faces
Jesus on the cross
Don Abrabanel
on the rack of the Inquisition
the rabbi of Lubavitch
booted in the mud
by brutish peasants

He closed his eyes
David's Star still bled
It is a sign for Easter Week
Christian blood
baked into those matzohs
they are required to eat
But he looked again
and knew
They are the same bloodless cakes
the Holy Son and his twelve apostles ate

He posed his hands in prayer
a comforting gesture

but in the afternoon glow
of the rose window
the ring of God glittered
He covered it
Who is to tell me
I am responsible
I make decisions
my wishes are executed
If I refuse to decide
their extermination will continue

"*Va a mori ammazzato*
As a child on the Rialto
I heard him curse my father
A Jew to wish my father dead?
Descendant of Shylock
Infidel pig
I'll have his head
his blood
their blood
Va a mori ammazzato
Let them die"

The Wandering Jew

The Wandering Jew on my window sill
Desperately needs new soil
Remembering it had struggled well
In its temporary home
I begin to replant a metaphor

The Wandering Jew of the Middle Ages
Legendary nomad I had just
Been writing a paper about
Flaming crosses   hooded cloaks
A Ku Klux Klan rally transported back
Nine hundred years
Cartaphilus   Shylock   all the wandering Abrahams
Owning nothing but
The pound of flesh
They had wedged between their teeth

The end of wandering
In families of burning flesh
The gold removed
From the teeth of this century

My fingers covered with dirt
I try to cover my mouth
I am gagging
On these thorns of Christian history

Christmas Vacation 1970/71

to Mike Eskolsky d. 10/16/71

"*Rage, Rage*" beseeches Thomas
"*against the dying of the light*"
and in the percussive carillon of your voice
there are no plangent emphysemic wheezings
Each remembered word an echoed mallet
pounding against my grief-worn brain

Even this book—his *Collected Poems*
your gift to me when I
was in the hospital having
my tonsils removed (at eighteen
nothing too serious)
"*Rage, rage . . .*" Thomas' impassioned chorus
reassures me you are at last
heeding a wiser man's advice

No man had ever
gifted me with poems before
and through the years
no other men as you played

father   brother   teacher   husband
and almost once my lover
The clue you said is in
the roles I play
But for seven years if you
disagreed with my choice of cast
you acquiesced in a none too subtle request
that you help direct my life

What did you ever
ask of me except that I
come south stay a week
and say goodbye   in New
York it is still winter for me
always the season of death every
thing seems glittered in frozen images

Does each impossible effort of breath
press upon your brain to release
another passionate reel of images
At dusk rushing to the hospital
sitting rigid on your bed
a healthy young woman slowly
growing old impotently listening
to you rage against your helplessness
And for all my lonely years ahead
you lovingly raged at me

In the final drama of death
there is no role to play
I listened grateful even for
an angry message my mother
died so passively even her poems
were somehow buried with her
You knew this and never
let the silence intervene

Afterwards in your almost bare apartment
finding small scholar's comfort
in your valuable collection of books
Baron Corvo   James Joyce
knowing it will take me years
to read them again alone
In New York David and I
had to divide the rest
of your library   two unwise Solomons
deciding how the child
might be best destroyed
On your balcony overlooking
that hospital city sterile white Miami
a new role set in the
tragic heroine wishing gin might kill

Each remembered word a mallet
"You must work through

the clichés of your life. . . . You
don't love yourself enough
. . . Disgust me? Baby you
don't know what love is"

"*Rage, rage . . .*" there is no
strength left in me
to rage against your dying never
loving life enough you know I
would probably die more softly
Loving you this much I came
to watch you die and there
were moments you had
to hate me for it
In New York it is
still winter for me appropriately
still the season of death

On the Wagon

They came to Abraham Lincoln to complain of General
Grant's drinking. "Really?" asked Lincoln. "Tell me, what
brand does he drink? I'd like to send some to the rest of my
generals."

Poets have been getting sick.
Lately their livers swelling to diseased size.
John Logan in my living room:
"I'm writing a poem
to my liver which doesn't read the papers
to know it can be transplanted."

Joel Oppenheimer—tonight the usual glass
first time at a reading filled with water.
Still, he reads with love and humor
but his face has lost its boyish wisdom.
What was carved, it seemed, in Black Mountain
granite now reworked in New York pain.

Poets have been getting sick.
In another year this room—
Poetry Center of the 92nd St. Y
will be open only during visiting hours.

And ink-stained doctors
will greet us at the doors.

Poets have been getting sick
and lately all our words are telling lies.
Grey-dimmed falseness of *The New York Times*
so fat, so richly healthy, describing how the
hearts of poets might be preserved in alcohol.

Borges Reading

April 5, 1971

At a movie I am
lost no need for com-
pany sometimes just a man's
shoulder to lean on

At a concert the eye
losing interest the other I
quickly carried into years
of dreams it never matters
who is sitting there

At a reading all senses
alert waiting to be fed
too often just a fast-ending
feast of words which deaden

But Borges   Borges blind
traveling light years in
his mind   his mind the
mirror for the passion
in his soul   creating magic
tigers hunting through the jungle

It is right she and I
am completely here no other
self wishing for another self
to understand the other
self who walks with Borges

He has made us feel
he really walks in all
of us this is the labyrinth
she told me I might
someday want to wander in

Out of the Desert

All that time wasted
wandering the Sinai of
my false idea
thinking I had to bring you
the magic of manna the
ingenuity of those wonderful cakes
(nourishing but tasteless)

And like the whore of Givah
twelve vital parts of her
distributed tribe by tribe
I thought that's how
you'd take me
Would you be Judah
and ask for the head
Or Reuben and ask
for the heart
Or Levi who took
nothing but knew
how to divide

Having no ritual
secret of survival

I bring you
this naked woman
having led herself
out of the desert

The Family

My father had six
brothers and sisters his own
father founding one of the
first schools of its kind
in a small town in Connecticut
And one day his wife my
grandmother went to take in
the mail and from a small brown
package leaped at her a small
dead rat   In that small town
in Connecticut she spent the rest
of her life in an institution

And her husband one of the finest
speakers in the State began
to stop talking slowly
dying from brain cancer and
my father was then a young man
in Poland witnessing his first pogrom
and trying to get home in time for
his father's funeral missed the boat

And a few years later he
married my mother her own
father a customer peddler on
the Lower East Side who after
twenty years was going to take a
vacation and left the key
to his safe with his eldest
son who promptly stole down to
the basement and took his last cent
And her youngest brother took
a bottle of bleach and dyed
all his hair blonde and their
mother my grandmother went swimming in
Far Rockaway in order to drown my
own mother from then on beginning
to drown in a sea of depression

And my father and mother stayed in
this small town in Connecticut which has
probably never been too conducive
to sanity and one night I imagine
my mother put me to sleep kissed me
on the cheek went into her room
put herself to sleep so that
my father had to climb through
the kitchen window in order to find

her dead in her bed and slowly
every black hair of his head
began to turn grey   I began
to grow older and watch them
craze into age my mother's
older brother selling elixir from
his home in Far Rockaway after
stealing my inheritance his younger
brother an uncle I love married
ten years rarely touching his
wife   My father's eldest sister
dying last year mourning her inability
to wear a new dress his other
sister dying in an institution
committed by her husband who
remarried two weeks later   A third
sister released years ago wandering
Miami and everyone glad they never
hear from her   her one living
sister too depressed now
to answer the phone

And just this week my cousin Bernie
died months after a nervous break
down his wife calling for help an uncle
who just last year had tried to seduce her

Only one brother who married off his son
to a girl he met twice and a sister
my aunt who doesn't answer the
phone attended the funeral   I had
asked my father not to come in
Is his family dying from a
contagious disease   My brother and
cousins have all run off with their
lovers   I feel I must stay in New York
to record this history

The Door Is Jammed Again

The door is jammed again
Which leaves me
To repeat an old cliché
Every lock has its key
Everything one does
Requires a method
But the door is
Jammed again

There is a history here
Of childhood murderers
My grandfather was a noted scholar
His seven children
Were and are
All failures

My father
Leaves me a heritage
of mismanaged love
He lost his wife
Then another
Bankrupt of

His son
His daughter

I tumble through relationships
Or like a burglar try to
Bore my way through the
Cold steel of their impenetrable core
My father
Rabbi preacher counselor locksmith
Reminds me
That I failed at
Geometry

Can one ever be sure
That in a relationship
The labyrinth
Is worthwhile enough to explore
The question
Like the key
Has long been bent
Out of shape

What comes naturally
Is loss
This has no method
Mechanical objects
Leave me hopeless

Intellectual images
Leave me worried
The rest leaves me shaking
And fumbling for the keys

"So much depends . . ."

"So much depends upon a
red wheel barrow"
Forgive me Dr. Williams
for rushing
through
your line breaks
Around here
so much depends
upon my
inner nature

One false move
and the scene
becomes a battlefield
Get the phone
off the hook
(the receiver
feels like
a rifle butt)
Jam the bell
(the enemy comes

a neighbor
with a problem)
Kill any human sound
with music

So funny
how closely related
to murder
is the impulse
to describe even
a red wheel barrow
glazed with rain water
beside the white chickens

Friday Night Yoga

It's just about that time
the men are proud and determined
hurrying to evening prayer
And I sneak into the Yoga center
at first ashamed
that this is how I greet you

Om shanti   shanti   shanti
Peace to the world
Good Shabbos God   Good Shabbos
I give to you as kiddush
my sun worship posture

They say that in each generation
old wine appears in new vessels
my self then
erect and proud
now strains to hold that wine

What I learn here tonight
stretching higher than I have
in years

is that we meet most earnestly
at awkward moments
in the strangest temples
Om shanti   shanti   shanti
Shabbat Shalom

IV

Never attend a wedding without/an escort...

The Wedding

Never attend a wedding without
an escort no matter
who he is or what he's
really like just
make certain he is
wearing a jacket and slacks
and a clean shirt and an
appropriate tie.   Dress him
yourself if you have to re
membering first to throw him
in the shower and to dash him
with English Leather so that he
smells good enough to
take anywhere.

Be there on time and
hold hands and smile at
each other content enough to
have with you a man who
stands on his own two feet just
like the man going down the aisle.

8

At the table of strangers you
need not speak to anyone you
have him to turn to and damn it
he smells great and that night if
you want to you may say good
night or have him stay till morning.

Mazel Tov

After nine months
we've given birth
to this
our wedding
made love in every
protected way
our only offspring
here under the *chupah*
shards of broken glass

After Selecting the Wedding Invitations

Last night
after selecting the wedding invitations
(the Hebrew lettering seemed fitting
signs of a Quamran Mystic
but David Empire Royal
goes better with Park Avenue)
we went looking for a poem
to celebrate
our printed commitment

Feast of Saint Gennaro
melange of variegated pork
and petty profiteering
Carnival crowds pushing through
the streets reflected in
shallow pools of sewaged olive oil

An aging couple
dancing on the sidewalk
Italian tarentella
I saw horas

and kazatzkas
my wedding
wondering
will we be this happy
dancing freely   openly
a poem after all
the edited stanzas of life

Last night I dreamed
a cat with ivory claws
attacked me

Wedding Day Dream

Most of a marriage
Takes place in the kitchen
On the day of my wedding
The dishes in the sink
Rise and fall like hailstones
It rains
My dreams freeze
Like Japanese buds
On a porcelain dish

You and I are hiding
Huddled near the stove
Looking for warmth
Hiding from relations
Crowding our house
With their marriages
Their offspring

Someone always finds us
Your mother
My cousin

It doesn't really matter
Who admonishes us
In our underwear
Why this   why here
Get ready
It's time   no time

Our love cannot hold
This last delay
Nor can it repel
The dripping seeping
Sounds of an unproved future

I enter alone
Meet you   a stranger
Yet this ritual
Ends the rain
On the day of our wedding
The sun almost shines

Letter to My Analyst

Are you interested in domestic crimes
The kind that never make the papers
Are recorded only in the
Marriage Histories
The Manuals of Marital Mystery
The misdemeanors—her crimes
The felonies—his

Last night my husband
Cleaned my desk
A felony
Sentenced by my imaginary judge
To years of imprisonment without me
This morning
Trying to work amidst
His tidiness
I want a divorce

In return
I watched the Late Show
Ignored his warnings
Empty threats the criminal repeats

When his crime is repaid
"I'm going to sleep"
A misdemeanor and
I was fined
One restless night

How could I
Make love to the man
Who buried my books
Filed my private papers
Stole my clean carbons
Destroyed my chaos from which
I rise desiring sex
And a neat man's
Other charms

Dreaming of Conn-Eda

The moral of the Story of Conn-Eda is: "follow your
unconscious intuitive forces blindly and with confident faith;
they will carry you through your perilous trials. Cherish them;
believe in them; do not frustrate them with intellectual distrust
and criticism; but permit them to move and sustain you."
                    Heinrich Zimmer: *The King and the Corpse*

Conn-Eda hid himself in horse's hide
thus warding off the dangers beyond the gate
It was easier in pagan legends
We have God   the death of God
ritual and life with no ritual
less innocence and more evil
What covers us is our own flesh
and less than gates hold back the danger

I am thinking of removing coverings
of tearing wide the curtain
gauze netting   cheese cloth mesh
a flimsy thing in which the knots get tighter
I am thinking of embracing my darkness
There is danger there
other levels   other depths

Here in my marriage bed
I am covered by a quilt
sewn with sinews I have discarded
made of skins I have flayed
throughout these years of revelation

I am thinking of Conn-Eda
I am dreaming of Conn-Eda
I am thinking of removing coverings
One has been shielding a seductive light
The other has been kept in the sun too long

There is a nighttime draft I can feel
through the places where the skins have cracked
Conn-Eda kisses me good-night
My husband sighs in his sleep
and covers my sex with his leg
I am dreaming of Conn-Eda

Tisha b'Av 1974

Here where the grass
grows like wheat
after ten years
I have come to fast
To share within this public ritual
my private destruction
my husband having left me
removing from my temple
stone upon stone

You come as our guest
to break this fast
and stay with me
until the cock crows once
Five thousand years ago
the Temple was still burning
Some time during this night
we have offered each other
our private flames

U

In this highly accessible collection of her poetry, Diane Levenberg speaks with both painful honesty and humor. With poignant, often startling images, she reveals her cultural and religious background, her joy and sadness, disappointments and dreams.

Often trying to find herself within the troubling course of her people's history, she is forced to battle the tempests of her own past. Her caravan through the desert is a colorful panoply of people, places, traumatic events. While drawing readers into unique personal situations, she compels them to recognize themselves in her experience, making her message inspiring and profound.

OUT OF THE DESERT is an intelligent and heartening book that, despite the pain it explores, looks for love and discovers hope.